TOGETHER

COMMUNITY THAT MARKED
THE ACTS 2 CHURCH

Lifeway Press®
Brentwood, Tennessee

EDITORIAL TEAM

Cynthia Hopkins
Writer

Jon Rodda
Art Director

Reid Patton
Senior Editor

Tyler Quillet
Managing Editor

Brett McIntosh
Associate Editor

Joel Polk
Publisher, Small Group Publishing

Katie Vogel
Assistant Editor

John Paul Basham
Director, Adult Ministry Publishing

Published by Lifeway Press® • © 2024 Ben Mandrell

ISBN 979-8-3845-1080-2 • Item 005849708

Dewey decimal classification: 262.7
Subject headings: CHRISTIAN LIFE \ CHURCH \ CHURCH FELLOWSHIP

Unless otherwise noted, all Scripture quotations are taken from the Christian Standard Bible®, Copyright © 2017 by Holman Bible Publishers. Used by permission. Christian Standard Bible® and CSB® are federally registered trademarks of Holman Bible Publishers. Scripture quotations marked (NIV) are taken from the Holy Bible, New International Version®, NIV®. Copyright © 1973, 1978, 1984, 2011 by Biblica, Inc.® Used by permission of Zondervan. All rights reserved worldwide. www.zondervan.com The "NIV" and "New International Version" are trademarks registered in the United States Patent and Trademark Office by Biblica, Inc.®

To order additional copies of this resource, write to Lifeway Resources Customer Service; 200 Powell Place, Suite 100; Brentwood, TN 37027-7707; fax 615-251-5933; call toll free 800-458-2772; order online at lifeway.com; email orderentry@lifeway.com.

Printed in the United States of America

Adult Ministry Publishing • Lifeway Resources
200 Powell Place, Suite 100 • Brentwood, TN 37027-7707

CONTENTS

ABOUT THE AUTHOR

Ben Mandrell is the president and CEO of Lifeway Christian Resources. Prior to coming to Lifeway, he pastored churches in Tennessee and Colorado. His pastor's heart and immense love for the church continue to be the clear motivations by which he leads. Ben preaches all over the United States and serves as a speaker at conferences and leadership/training events. With his wife, Lynley, he co-hosts *The Glass House* podcast—conversations that help cultivate healthy emotions and relationships for ministry leaders and their families.

HOW TO USE THIS STUDY

This Bible study provides a guided process for individuals and small groups to experience the uniquely necessary and uncommon togetherness of Christian community. Six sessions of study work through the applications of life together in Christ. The prayer for this study is that God will set new relational expectations among believers in local churches and foster a desire in individual believers to personally engage in Christian community according to those expectations.

GROUP STUDY

Regardless of what day of the week your group meets, each session of content begins with the group session. Each group session uses the following format to facilitate simple yet meaningful interaction among group members and with God's Word.

START

The group session will begin with a few questions designed to help you introduce the session's topic of study and encourage everyone to engage with the study.

WATCH

This section provides key statements from the video teaching, as well as blank space for you to take notes. Codes to access the teaching videos are included with your purchase of this book and can be found on the insert located at the back of the book.

DISCUSS

This section is the main component of the group session. The questions provided are designed to facilitate the group study of the session's topic. The goal is to help you better understand the community that marked the Acts 2 church and begin to personally relate to others that way in your local church context.

PERSONAL STUDY

Each group study is followed by the opportunity to reflect on the personal context you bring to the session's topic, two days of personal Bible study to help you think biblically about the topic, and a follow-up opportunity to help you personally respond to the topic. With biblical teaching and introspective questions, these segments work together to challenge you to grow in your understanding of God's Word and respond in faith and obedience.

PERSONAL CONTEXT

The personal study section begins with an opportunity to identify certain life lessons that have impacted your current views and relational practices in the community of faith. This will help you identify ways you struggle with the truth and approach the biblical text understanding your personal need.

PERSONAL BIBLE STUDY 1 AND 2

The group and personal studies are complementary. These studies are meant to deepen your understanding of togetherness among believers and help you reflect upon and apply what you learn in the group session.

PERSONAL RESPONSE

The personal study section ends with questions that call attention to areas of focus for changes you need to make going forward.

TIPS FOR LEADING A SMALL GROUP

Follow these guidelines to prepare for each group session.

PRAYERFULLY PREPARE

Review the weekly material and group questions ahead of time. Be intentional about praying for each person in the group. Ask the Holy Spirit to work through you and the group discussion as you point your small group to Jesus each week through God's Word.

MINIMIZE DISTRACTIONS

Create a comfortable environment. If group members are uncomfortable, they'll be distracted and, therefore, not engaged in the group experience. Plan ahead by considering details like seating, temperature, lighting, food and drink, surrounding noise, and general cleanliness.

Thoughtfulness and hospitality show guests and group members they're welcome and valued in whatever environment you choose to gather. Some people may not notice your effort, but your preparation will help elimate distractions. Do everything in your ability to help people focus on what's most important: connecting with God, with the Bible, and with one another.

INCLUDE OTHERS

Your goal is to foster a community in which people are welcome just as they are but encouraged to grow spiritually. Always be aware of opportunities to invite new people to join your group and to include any visitors in the discussion. An inexpensive way to invite someone to get involved or to make first-time guests feel welcome is to give them their own copies of this Bible study book.

ENCOURAGE DISCUSSION

A good small group experience has the following characteristics.

EVERYONE PARTICIPATES. Encourage everyone to ask questions, share responses, or read aloud.

NO ONE DOMINATES—NOT EVEN THE LEADER. Be sure that your time speaking as a leader takes up less than half of your time together as a group. Politely guide discussion if anyone dominates.

NOBODY IS RUSHED THROUGH QUESTIONS. Don't feel that a moment of silence is a bad thing. People often need time to think about their responses to questions they've just heard or to gain courage to share what God is stirring in their hearts.

INPUT IS AFFIRMED AND FOLLOWED UP WITH ADDITIONAL DISCUSSION. Make sure you point out something true or helpful in a response. Don't just move on. Build community with follow-up questions, asking how other people have experienced similar things or how a truth has shaped their understanding of God and the Scripture you're studying. People are less likely to speak up if they are afraid you don't actually want to hear their answers or think you're looking for only a certain answer.

GOD AND HIS WORD ARE CENTRAL. Opinions and experiences can be helpful, but God has given us the truth. Trust Scripture to be the authority and God's Spirit to work in people's lives. You can't change anyone, but God can. Continually point people to the Word and to active steps of faith.

KEEP CONNECTING

Think of ways to connect with group members during the week. Participation during the group session is always improved when members spend time connecting with one another outside the group sessions. The more people are comfortable with and involved in one another's lives, the more they'll look forward to being together. When people move beyond being friendly to truly being friends who form a community, they come to each session eager to engage instead of merely attending. When possible, build deeper friendships outside your regularly scheduled group time by planning a gathering or spontaneously inviting group members to join you for meals, fun activities, or projects around your home, church, or community.

SEEING

GOD'S

VISION

TRUTH

Community is a
defining marker
of New Testament
Christianity.

GROUP STUDY

START

Welcome to session 1 of Together, *"Seeing God's Vision."*

Before you dive into the group study, introduce yourselves and share one reason why you decided to join this study on togetherness in the church.

In each week of our study, we'll see God's vision for our lives together in the church through the example of the very first church in Acts 2. Jesus had promised the Holy Spirit would come, but before that happened, these believers were a pretty dysfunctional group. They had trust issues. They had anxiety and fear. They didn't really know how to do life together. But then, the Holy Spirit came like Jesus promised, and everything changed. Peter boldly preached the gospel to people from all over the world who had come to Jerusalem for Passover. The Spirit was at work in, through, and around them all.

READ ACTS 2:41-47. What do you see in the experience and example of the very first church that you want to see in the context of church life today?

Community is a defining marker of New Testament Christianity.

Is there anything from their experience and example that, if it happened in your local church, would make you a little uncomfortable? Why?

Obviously, we live in a different time and a different culture than we read about in Acts 2. We're *together* in different circumstances. But God's vision for His church today is the same as it was for the early church in its very first days. As He was then, the Holy Spirit is at work now—in us, through us, and around us. The question is, will we open ourselves up to Him as He does that work?

To prepare for the video teaching, pray together and ask God to help each person understand and apply this truth.

WATCH

*Use these statements to follow along as you watch the video teaching
for session 1, and use the blank space to take additional notes.*

There are four very clear pillars—the vision—that God put forth for the church:
teaching, fellowship, forgiveness, and prayer.

ACTS 2:42

Authentic community is only going to happen if you bring the real you.

Every one of these four foundations requires an enormous amount of courage.

To access the video teaching sessions,
use the instructions in the back
of your Bible study book.

GROUP STUDY

DISCUSS

Use these questions and prompts to discuss the video teaching.

What stood out to you personally in Ben's teaching?

What has been your attitude or perspective about the future of the local church lately? What hopes do you have for the future of the local church?

Would you say you're relating to others in the church in a way that aligns with God's vision for those relationships? Why?

Whatever lesser realities the local church has accepted instead of the greater reality God envisions are important to identify. But those lesser realities do not need to define the future of our faith communities. God's vision for the church today is the same as it was for the first church that came on the scene after Jesus died, rose, ascended to heaven, and sent His Spirit to indwell all who believe in Him. And that vision is realized through our devotion to the four pillars He set before us in the example of the early church in Acts 2:42—teaching, fellowship, the breaking of bread (forgiveness), and prayer.

Which of the four pillars of the church—teaching, fellowship, forgiveness, and prayer—is your heart most drawn to? Why?

Which one do you struggle with most? How so?

There were numerous good pursuits the first church could have chosen to devote themselves to. The needs of this overnight megachurch were certainly many. What worship songs would they sing now that they knew salvation had come in Jesus Christ? Who would lead kids' ministry? And many of those pursuits would have surely been easier. But prioritizing those pursuits over devotion to teaching, fellowship, forgiveness, and prayer would have neglected what was *best*.

Why is devotion to biblical teaching critical to the health of the church body? What about fellowship? Forgiveness? Prayer?

Ben said, "Authentic community is only going to happen if you bring the real you." How does our willingness to be real with each other in the church impact the effectiveness of the four pillars of the church?

Ben's story about pastoring churches and then realizing that very few people, if any, really knew him illuminates the lack of authenticity many of us experience and accept in the context of the local church. It's easier to do church activities than it is to *be* the church in relational vulnerability. God's vision, though, is that we each bring our real selves every time we gather.

Why do you think we often struggle to be real about our needs—whether we need wisdom, support, provision, or help facing temptation or overcoming sin—as we gather together in the community of faith?

Ben said it takes enormous courage to see past the fear and awkwardness to walk in the clarity of God's vision for the church. In regard to the four pillars lived out as our model in Acts 2:42, where do you need courage?

Name a few steps we each can take to help the local fellowship of believers see God's vision for the church and walk in it.

CLOSE IN PRAYER

Where I Am

Every church attendee carries their own unique history, present circumstances, and future expectations that impact the way they understand the church and their role in it. Identifying those factors makes space for God to address, affirm, and correct them according to His Word. In *Together: Community That Marked the Acts 2 Church,* each week's personal study will give you the opportunity to identify how these factors impact your perspective.

Consider and respond to the prompts below in light of the question, "What is God's vision for the church?"

The view I inherited:

How my view has changed over time:

Factors that have shaped my view:

Reasons I have sometimes been discouraged:

Questions I have:

Search me, God, and know my heart;
test me and know my concerns.
See if there is any offensive way in me;
lead me in the everlasting way.
PSALM 139:23-24

What Scripture Teaches

"May they all be one, as you, Father, are in me and I am in you.
May they also be in us, so that the world may believe you sent me."
JOHN 17:21

While our personal histories might at times cloud our view of the local church, God's vision remains crystal clear. Jesus prayed that all believers would be together, as one, in Him. His vision is that our unity would be palpable in every generation and culture, like stars shining brightly in the darkest night sky.

What are some groups or places in your life where there is a strong sense of community?

How did that unity develop?

How is God's vision for unity in the church different than the unity you find in your neighborhood, work, or civic organizations?

The unity experienced in the church is unique. It isn't built on a political ideology, a career path, a favorite football team, or a love of Mexican food or pickle ball! It doesn't depend on our agreement on every matter. No one is excluded because of their background, personality, culture, or race.

And that incredible bond of unity will be the eternal reality for every person who trusts in Jesus Christ. The innumerable multitude of believers "from every nation, tribe, people, and language" will stand together "before the throne and before the Lamb," crying out praises to Him in perfect unity (Revelation 7:9-10).

> If unity among believers is an ultimate, eternal reality, then why was Jesus concerned enough to pray about it in John 17?

Togetherness in Christ is an inevitable eternal outcome. Yet it has no earthly guarantee.

Our human nature conflicts with life in the Spirit. We live in a world filled with loneliness, isolation, unrest, and individualism. Even the most faithful believers struggle to reflect eternal realities in relationships here on earth. That is as true today as it was when Jesus prayed for unity in John 17.

So how can God's vision for His church be carried out by sinful people here on this sin-cursed earth? No perfect church exists. Yet God equipped and empowered the first church, in part, to provide a working model for the rest of us to follow. Their example is God's design for our churches.

READ ACTS 2:36-47.

> *They devoted themselves to the apostles' teaching, to the fellowship, to the breaking of bread, and to prayer.*
> **ACTS 2:42**

The first church to gather after Jesus's death, resurrection, and ascension is a picture of God's vision for all local churches in every generation. They weren't perfect—they were flawed people just like us. But when they turned to Jesus in faith and the Spirit began to work in them and among them, everything changed. These flawed people, most of whom had previously abandoned or rejected Jesus altogether, experienced a radical reframing of unity and commitment.

In tomorrow's study, we'll zoom in and take a look at the practical applications of their newfound unity and commitment in detail. Today, however, let's take a 30,000-foot view of the early church model.

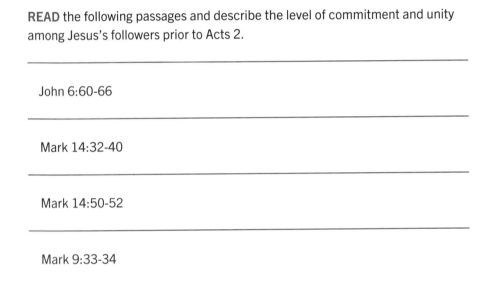

READ the following passages and describe the level of commitment and unity among Jesus's followers prior to Acts 2.

John 6:60-66

Mark 14:32-40

Mark 14:50-52

Mark 9:33-34

NOW REREAD ACTS 2:36-47. Describe the commitment and unity of Jesus's followers in the first church. What was different now?

Based on the Acts 2 church model, what is possible for your local church?

When the Holy Spirit indwelt the members of the first church, His next act was to reframe their understanding of unity, family, and commitment. Their experience is our example, preserved in God's Word to reframe our expectations some 2,000 years later.

We live in an easy-bake culture where investments of time and commitment are seen as tying us down and limiting our options. This approach to life has bled into the church. The reality, though, is that commitment to the church is the only way we can experience the full benefits of the church.

What is your responsibility in carrying out God's vision for the church?

We learn in Acts 2 that people couldn't stay away. The devotion among believers to God and each other was so compelling that outsiders came to faith and joined their group each and every day. As they did, those new members joined God's people in living out the beautiful, though imperfect, expression of God's vision for His church.

This was not simply a reality God intended to occur one time and one time only. He means for His church to experience it at every moment. He means for *you* to experience it now.

We will find the fullest expression of the Holy Spirit's power when we are most closely aligned to God's design. Then, we will experience community unlike any other.

What Scripture Teaches

Everyone was filled with awe, and many wonders and signs were being performed through the apostles. Now all the believers were together and held all things in common.
ACTS 2:43-44

If the first church had a website, the tagline "Together" would have absolutely been on brand. The community of faith in its earliest days would serve as the standard for every additional local church going forward.

REREAD ACTS 2:42. What was the basis of their unity?

When you work on a puzzle, the job becomes 100 times easier if you look at the top of the box. The puzzle maker has given you a picture of what it's supposed to look like. You are not creating something in the dark.

Similarly, God has not left us without the top of the box when it comes to church. Local churches all look and feel a little different because people are unique and so are their cultures, but God's design for a healthy church does not change. Acts 2:42 gives us the picture we are to emulate. God's vision for every body of believers involves commitment from its members to engage together in gospel teaching, fellowship, forgiveness, and prayer. And these four components for church health should be seen in all of the diverse congregations scattered across the globe. Let's take a look at each aspect of devotion shared by members of the first church in greater depth.

They were a learning community.

The day Jesus announced Himself as the Messiah, He went to the synagogue, which was the place of public learning. There, He unrolled the scroll of Isaiah and read aloud the ancient words of God (Luke 4:16-19). Jesus never stopped giving learning opportunities to anyone within earshot. From sermons and stories for large crowds to private tutorials for a select few, Jesus was devoted to teaching—and the church continued to follow His example as they "devoted themselves to the apostles' teaching" (Acts 2:42).

What do these verses communicate about the priority of teaching and learning gospel truths?

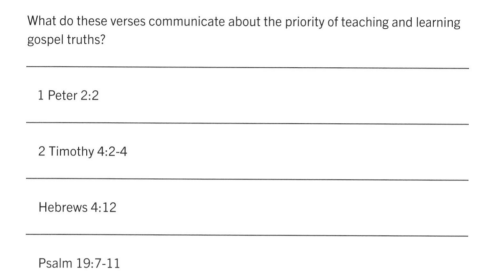

1 Peter 2:2

2 Timothy 4:2-4

Hebrews 4:12

Psalm 19:7-11

Teaching and learning should always hold a prominent place in our churches. When a baby is delivered into the world, the first thing he or she needs is nourishment. When a brand new Christian is born, the first thing he or she needs is teaching. And like the infant's relationship with milk and nourishment, that need will never end! Even the most mature saints among us devote themselves to continual learning.

The early church was a thoughtful community—and that is God's design for every local church. As we learn from God's Word, we grow spiritually as individuals and *together*, unifying the church around His truth and through His love.

How has God energized you lately through the teaching of His Word in your local church?

They were a caring and sharing community.

The commitment the first Christians had to each other is striking. In fact, the direct application of Acts 2:44-45 in church life today feels so mind-boggling that many prefer to dismiss it rather than emulate it.

In the original language of the New Testament, the word for *fellowship* in verse 42 means "close association involving mutual interests and sharing."[1] In other words, "fellowship" means more than "they liked to hang out" or "they enjoyed grabbing coffee." The relationships in this community involved willing, voluntary sacrifice (vv. 44-45). Galatians 6 offers us additional insight.

> **READ GALATIANS 6:10.** List any words or phrases that are instructive to you. How does this verse help you understand God's design for fellowship?

> When have you seen the commitment to caring and sharing demonstrated in church life? How does the willingness to share needs and meet needs unify the church?

They were a forgiveness-first community.

Just as the early church's devotion to fellowship was about far more than hanging out at a local taco stand, so was their devotion to the "breaking of bread" (Acts 2:42). They gathered in each other's houses regularly, even daily, to eat "with joyful and sincere hearts" (v. 46). These meals would often end in remembering Jesus's death and resurrection as they took the Lord's Supper together. The broken bread and the sip of wine were symbolic of Jesus's shattered body and spilled blood, poured out for our sins.

> In what way does the "breaking of bread" in communion unify the church?

---

1. William Arndt et al., A Greek-English Lexicon of the New Testament and Other Early Christian Literature (Chicago: University of Chicago Press, 2000), 552.

Breaking bread "from house to house" (v. 46) gives the sense of an intimate, informal practice of recentering life on the gospel through our shared relationship with Jesus and our communal relationship with each other. The conscious act of confessing sin acknowledges the need for sustaining grace. The early Christians took the Lord's Supper (also called Communion) together—not out of need for ritual but out of a desperate desire for felt forgiveness.

> **READ JAMES 5:16.** Respond to the following idea: No sacrifice you make for the Lord is greater than your readiness to set others free from their offenses.

The first church, which serves as our model of God's design, took the Lord's Supper as a meaningful and tangible reminder of the grace they had received from God and the grace they were called to extend to each other. The continual practice of grace and forgiveness solidified their unity—and it will solidify ours today.

They were a praying community.

> Have you experienced prayer as a unifying force in your local church? Why does prayer have that effect?

As important as friendships were, the early believers understood the health of their faith community would be determined by the strength of their connection to God—so they devoted themselves to prayer (Acts 2:42). When conversation with God is interrupted, it does not take long for relationships to be interrupted with feelings of apathy or even anger at other people. On the other hand, the stronger your vertical fellowship is, the stronger your horizontal fellowship will be.

Why were the members of the first church devoted in these four ways? They were obedient to the call to be the church. What about you? Will you be devoted to learning, sharing and caring, forgiving, and praying in the context of a local body of believers? Living within God's design isn't casual, it is living in the way of Jesus.

Where I'm Going

For the church to be healthy, every single person has to take responsibility for the four areas of devotion the early church demonstrated in Acts 2:42. In other words, the Christian faith, which is lived out in church community, is something to be practiced—you have to continually work at it. Just like an athlete who stops practicing will lose his or her edge, the Christian who neglects one of these four key areas will suffer and hold the church back from operating fully in God's design.

Consider each area of your commitment to the local church, and record steps you can take to move forward as a devoted member.

They devoted themselves to the apostles' teaching,

What are you doing to grow your mind toward God?

What one step can you take to expand your learning this week?

. . . to the fellowship,

Are you making room in your life for relationships to grow into authentic friendships? Or are you skimming the surface of fellowship?

What one step can you take to develop your spiritual relationships?

. . . to the breaking of bread,

What one step can you take in your confession with other people?

. . . and to prayer.

What one step can you take to build your prayer life?

A little leaven leavens the whole batch of dough.
GALATIANS 5:9

SESSION 2

RELATING

AS

FAMILY

TRUTH

We are not intended
to walk alone,
and the local church
is the place where we
can find the closest
connections.

GROUP STUDY

START

Welcome to session 2 of Together, *"Relating As Family."*
Before you dive into the group study, take a few moments to review session 1.

Each week, before we dive into our new group study, we'll spend some time talking about insights we discovered through the previous week's personal study and response. The review questions will be simple, designed to help us press into what God's Word is teaching us about togetherness in the community of faith.

> What did you learn about God's vision for togetherness among believers in your study of Acts 2:36-47 and Jesus's prayer in John 17:21? Did this challenge your perspective on the purpose of the church? How?

> Name one step God is leading you to take to better see and live out His vision for the church in the days ahead.

We are not intended to walk alone, and the local church is the place where we can find the closest connections.

As we see God's vision for togetherness in the church, we are often tempted to become disillusioned by the ways churches are failing in that regard. Rather than devoting ourselves to the body through teaching, fellowship, forgiveness, and prayer, our inclination is to criticize leaders we deem solely responsible for this togetherness deficit. This is shortsighted. Everyone in the church needs to take ownership of these pillars. For togetherness to develop among us, individual believers must begin to relate to each other as family—because that is what we are.

To prepare for the video teaching, pray together and ask God to help each person understand and apply this truth.

WATCH

Use these statements to follow along as you watch the video teaching
for session 2, and use the blank space to take additional notes.

Are there people you've allowed into your fragility and need, connecting with so deeply that they'd be willing to carry you to Jesus?

MARK 2:1-12

Three things to notice in Mark 2:1-12:

      1. The faith of the people who bring their friend

      2. The compassion Jesus has for the broken

      3. The power of community

Friendliness and friendship are very different things. For us to experience community in the church, we have to go deeper than the exchange of pleasantries.

To access the video teaching sessions,
use the instructions in the back
of your Bible study book.

GROUP STUDY

DISCUSS

Use these questions and prompts to discuss the video teaching.

What stood out to you personally in Ben's teaching?

Ben said church is "supposed to be a place where you feel like people have your back," a place where you feel "safe and encouraged." In what sense should we have each other's backs?

How does our previous session's focus on authenticity help you understand safety and encouragement in church life?

READ MARK 2:1-12. Who in this passage had relationships that represent "having someone's back," safety, and encouragement? How so?

Who or what in the passage points to relationships where people were more interested in themselves than having someone else's back?

Though they knew the crowd and religious leaders who were present didn't relate to each other in safe or encouraging ways, the four friends were undeterred. They took initiative to go against cultural norms. They got their friend to Jesus, even though that wasn't how the larger group was relating to each other.

What are some norms in church culture today that serve as barriers we must cross if we're going to truly relate to one another as family?

When we think about togetherness in the church, it's easy to center those thoughts around our experiences with others and perceptions of those experiences. For example, you might judge a small group as shallow because the people in it never share struggles. But in this week's video teaching, we were challenged to address the problems of connecting with other believers by looking inwardly.

What do the actions of the four friends reveal to you about their understanding of community and their role as part of that community? What about Jesus's role in community?

Ben asked, "Are there people you've allowed into your fragility and need, connecting so deeply that they'd be willing to carry you to Jesus?" In what sense are healthy connections in the local church up to you?

Ben noted three things in the passage: the faith of the four friends, the compassion Jesus has for the broken, and the power of community.

What are the connections between these three things—our faith, Jesus's compassion, and the power of community—and relating together with other believers as family?

CLOSE IN PRAYER

Where I Am

God's vision for the church begins to flesh itself out in and among individuals who join with others in the gospel unity of belief in Jesus Christ. All Christians are family, and we will one day relate to each other perfectly as such. Here on earth, though, that family relationship is embodied within local churches filled with imperfect people from imperfect families. Those imperfections impact our understanding and expectations of what family should look like. To move toward a biblical understanding of the church as the family of God, we need to reckon with our own views of family.

Consider and respond to the prompts below in light of the question, "What should it feel like to be part of the family of God?"

The view I inherited:

How my view has changed over time:

Factors that have shaped my view:

Reasons I have sometimes been discouraged:

Questions I have:

Search me, God, and know my heart;
test me and know my concerns.
See if there is any offensive way in me;
lead me in the everlasting way.
PSALM 139:23-24

What Scripture Teaches

When you were in school, did you like group projects or hate them? Were you the kid who was glad to socialize and get help, or were you the kid who would much rather do it on your own and avoid people who might wreck your GPA? Teachers understand the tension that second kid feels, but they also know there's a deeper purpose to group work that's ultimately more important than the grade any one student gets at the end: We all need to learn how to live and work in community. That's how life is meant to be lived.

How does group work apply to spiritual life? What tension and/or sacrifice comes with uniting with other believers in ongoing, meaningful ways?

Note what each of the following verses teach about who we are in Christ.

John 1:12

Romans 12:5

Ephesians 2:19

All of us prefer our comfort zones, yet the Word of God says that human beings were designed by God to be relational creatures. Even though people can be disappointing, frustrating, and irritating at times, community is worth fighting for. Scripture makes it clear—in Christ, we are joined together. We are *family*.

And we are meant to experience that relationship as an ongoing, deepening reality. While it's nice to see a warm smile when you walk in the front door of the church, there's a longing for so much more inside every human soul. Every person, no matter how introverted by nature, desires a deeper connection with others that would include investment, sacrifice, and love.

They devoted themselves . . . to the fellowship.
ACTS 2:42

Compare your relationships within your local church to the example of the early church. In what ways are you devoted to the fellowship of a church family?

The commitment the early church made to each other drives home the importance of sincere, loving relationships with other believers. It challenges us to consider the profound sense of safety that comes from letting others care for us as family.

But relating to one another as family doesn't come naturally, and the early church members didn't invent that practice. In fact, if left up to their own nature, they wouldn't have done it at all. It's Jesus who makes us family.

READ MARK 2:1-12.

In this passage, Mark tells us that Jesus looked in three directions and saw three very different things—the exclusivity of the crowd, the irritation of the religious teachers, and the faithfulness of friends. We'll get to the good stuff in the next personal study, but for today, let's focus on the natural inclination of the crowd and the religious leaders that had gathered.

So many people gathered together that there was no more room,
not even in the doorway, and he was speaking the word to them . . .
they were not able to bring him to Jesus because of the crowd.
MARK 2:2,4a

Underline the part of the story in Mark 2:2 and 4a that might indicate the crowd was devoted to Jesus and one another. Circle the part of the story that indicates the large crowd represented something other than true devotion to Jesus and one another.

Why do you think the crowd of people didn't make a way for the paralyzed man and his friends to get through to Jesus?

Why aren't large crowds of people at church necessarily an indicator of spiritual health within that church?

Showing up matters. Numerical growth is one very real and important effect of the togetherness of heart and purpose shared by the early church (Acts 2:47). At the same time, we should not assume that crowds equal commitment to Jesus and one another. In Mark 2, there was no room at the door, and though a man in need was present, no one *made* any room at the door. The residents of Capernaum gathered around Jesus were a crowd, not a family.

Have you ever been to a church where you didn't feel like you could get "in" with people? What are some ways this kind of crowd mentality shows up in church life today?

Now, consider the religious insiders of Jesus's day. What was their take on this man's encounter with Jesus (vv. 6-8)?

*Right away Jesus perceived in his spirit that they were
thinking like this within themselves and said to them,
"Why are you thinking these things in your hearts?"*

MARK 2:8

While the crowd mentality outside forced the men to get creative in bringing their friend to Jesus, there was a clique inside the house that Jesus saw right through. The religious leaders were less interested in relationship with Jesus and others around them than they were in the rules and traditions they'd built their impressive lives upon. And it kept them from experiencing the grace of true togetherness.

Jesus sees our hangups and presuppositions—and He wants us to see them, too. Our lack of togetherness in the family of God rarely results from a lack of physical space or blasphemous teaching. The true barrier is our unwillingness to humbly consider others as more important than ourselves (Philippians 2:3-4).

Like the crowd blocking the door, we can get so caught up in what we want that we ignore the needs of other people. Or, like the religious leaders, we can get so caught up in what's familiar that we judge everyone else with cynicism. Both of those attitudes surface out of fear that if we let people in, we're going to lose our place, position, or preferences. We need to make room in our hearts, because crowd and clique mentalities block people from seeing and knowing Jesus.

Can you relate to the crowd mentality that was present in Mark 2:1-12?
The mentality of the cliquish scribes? How so?

*Jesus knows all the reasons we struggle
relationally. Still, His vision for each of us as part
of His church is the devotion of family.*

What Scripture Teaches

REREAD MARK 2:1-12.

In our previous personal study, we looked at two of the three people groups Jesus saw crammed shoulder to shoulder at the home where many had gathered to hear Him teach—the self-centered crowd and the hard-hearted scribes. Both groups help us recognize aspects of dysfunction that exist in many church families today. When we are inwardly focused, we become complacent about bringing people to Jesus and making disciples. When we allow our hearts to become closed off to God and His people, we become apathetic to the spiritual needs of others and miss gospel realities God wants us to see.

How was the mindset of the four who carried the paralyzed man different than the mindsets of the scribes and the crowd?

What obstacles could have stopped them from getting the man to Jesus?

We know nothing about the backstory. We don't know how these four came to know the paralyzed man or what relationships they shared with him. We do know they had faith—and together, they were unified in the purpose of bringing this man in need to Jesus. It wasn't easy; there were multiple obstacles in the way. But they were persistent because they believed it would be worth the effort.

How did Jesus respond to the men who brought the paralyzed man to Him? Why?

Note below the ways the five men related to Jesus, each other, and everyone else who had gathered as family. For each, write one way you can demonstrate that same quality in relationships within your local church.

Sticking together

Unity of purpose

Wanting what's best for each other

Serving each other

Vulnerability

Persistence

Courage to do what's right

Interdependence

Love

Sacrifice

Now, identify an obstacle that could keep you from relating to others as family in those ways.

It is a mystery how faith works. We are not provided a formula or a diagram, but the Bible is very clear that few things move the heart of Jesus like childlike faith. It's important that we have faith for ourselves—that each of us believes that "He who started a good work in you will carry it on to completion until the day of Christ Jesus" (Philippians 1:6). This is the fuel for waking up in the morning, even when life feels heavy and sad and impossible. Faith keeps us moving forward with our eyes on God, who walks with us through difficulty.

But notice that this passage isn't about the faith of the paralytic. When Jesus looked up, He saw something remarkable: four human beings who all believed Jesus could perform miracles. And the Bible says, because of "their faith," the man experienced a total overhaul of his soul and body. He not only picked up his mat, he left behind his shame and his guilt (vv. 5,11-12).

When has another person's faith helped you know Jesus's power in a circumstance where you were unable to stand in faith on your own?

Together, we can anticipate a miracle. Together, we wait to see what Jesus will do. Together, we trust that our sacrifices will be seen and rewarded by God.

Verses 9-12 call attention three times to Jesus's instruction to the man to take his mat with him. But the man was healed and no longer needed his mat. So why might Jesus have told him to take it with him?

This man couldn't deny his own limitations. He had no room for self-sufficiency or over-confidence. For as long as he'd been paralyzed, he'd had to rely on others for every-thing, and everyone who knew him knew his story. His life going forward, then, would be a living, breathing, walking testimony. His mat served as an object lesson—he'd been carried by the faith of his friends (who acted more like family) to a better future in Christ. And that story illuminates God's design for His church.

It's hard to hide limitations and ugly realities from family. They're usually the first to know them—maybe even before we know them ourselves. What does that kind of authentic relationship do for us in the body of Christ?

*Now all the believers were together
and held all things in common.*
ACTS 2:44

Acts 2:42 tells us the early church was devoted to fellowship. Verse 44 makes sure we don't undervalue that reality. Clearly, this commitment to community was more than a desire for potluck dinners and Super Bowl parties. Those early Christians felt fragile and afraid and were filled with normal, human doubts. They knew that their day of trouble was coming, that disappointment on earth was inevitable, but as long as they had strong relationships within God's family, they could carry each other through.

*Believing in God together empowers us to persevere
through life's most difficult moments.*

Where I'm Going

Our togetherness in the local church begins with the understanding that God makes us family. Like the very first church we read about in Acts 2:42, every believer in Christ today is called to a devoted relationship with Jesus and also to every person whose faith is in Him. When we are saved by Jesus, we are saved into Jesus's family.

Look back at your "Where I Am" responses on pages 38-39. Now, consider where God is leading you based on your study in Mark 2:1-12 this week.

They came to him bringing a paralytic, carried by four of them.
MARK 2:3

What is a situation that has (or has had) you feeling defeated and hopeless? Do you have a few people in your life whose faith can carry you? If so, who are they? If not, who are a few people you can start building that kind of relationship with?

What is a situation in which someone else needs you to carry them by faith? How can you do that?

Why are you thinking these things in your hearts?
MARK 2:8A

What situation or relationship has you operating with a cynical spirit toward other people or toward God, like the scribes in Jesus's day?

What should you do to address the cynicism in you?

Immediately he got up, took the mat,
and went out in front of everyone.
MARK 2:12A

Write your testimony of Jesus's work in your life, past and present.

Do you have a few meaningful friends in your local church who know your ongoing testimony of faith in Christ? How does sharing yourself in that way contribute to a sense of family among believers?

A little leaven leavens the whole batch of dough.
GALATIANS 5:9

BEING KNOWN AND LOVED

TRUTH

When we walk together
in sincerity, giving one
another permission to
not have it all together,
we are stronger.

GROUP STUDY

START

Welcome to session 3 of Together, *"Being Known and Loved."*
Before you dive into the group study, take a few moments to review session 2.

As we did last week, we want to spend some time talking about insights we discovered through the previous week's personal study and response. It's important for each of us to identify how we're going to apply the biblical truths we're learning to our own relationships in the body of Christ.

> What did you learn about relating as family with other believers in your study of Acts 2:42 and Mark 2:1-12?

> Name one step God is leading you to take so you can more genuinely relate to other believers as family in the days ahead.

When we walk together in sincerity, giving one another permission to not have it all together, we are stronger.

One of the greatest blessings of family is having people in your life who know you fully and love you completely. The same is true for the family of God. You are not *family* with others in your local church in name only. You are fully known and completely loved by God, and that individual, vertical reality is one that is meant to be shared horizontally in the community of faith.

How does this week's session title, "Being Known and Loved," strike you in terms of relationships in the local church (e.g., impossible, uncomfortable, personal experience, etc.)?

— *To prepare for the video teaching, pray together and ask God to help each person understand and apply this truth.*

WATCH

Use these statements to follow along as you watch the video teaching
for session 3, and use the blank space to take additional notes.

To be sincere means to not try to be impressive.

ACTS 2:46

The apostle Paul was not impressive. What we notice, instead, is his weakness.

1 CORINTHIANS 2:1

Paul was a better brother in Christ because he had walked through pain.

2 CORINTHIANS 12:7-10

What really brings people together in community is when they are unashamedly weak.

JAMES 5:16

To access the video teaching sessions,
use the instructions in the back
of your Bible study book.

GROUP STUDY

DISCUSS

Use these questions and prompts to discuss the video teaching.

What stood out to you personally in Ben's teaching?

READ ACTS 2:46-47. How did the first church relate to one another? How did the joyful sincerity they each brought to the table impact the community?

Ben defined the sincerity of heart relationally present in the early church as the decision "to not try to be impressive." Let's think about that more deeply than we might if we just quickly read through these verses. Beyond all our *doing* in the world (career successes, children's accomplishments, etc.), there are many ways we try to be impressive—withholding our struggles, avoiding engaging with others in their struggles, and never voicing our worries, to name a few.

Name one relational context where it's it difficult for you to personally relate in sincerity (e.g., at work, in conversations with your pastor or another respected church leader, in a small group like this one). Why do you keep people in that social context at a distance?

Can any of us be known and loved in the local church without sincerity? Why?

Who is someone you experience as a sincere person among the community of faith? Would you say sincerity of heart is something you commonly encounter in relationships in the church?

The believers in the early church doubtlessly had the same reasons we have for not letting others see our true selves. Even the apostle Paul was tempted to think more highly of himself than he ought and to project that ideal image to others.

READ 2 CORINTHIANS 12:7-10. What was the purpose of the struggle God allowed Paul to experience?

What was Paul's purpose in sharing his weakness with other Christians?

The truth highlighted at the beginning of this session says, "When we walk together in sincerity, giving one another permission to not have it all together, we are stronger." That strength is experienced both individually and communally. God allowed Paul to experience weakness so that He could give Paul strength. Paul acknowledged His weakness to experience Christ's strength. The community of faith then and now has found encouragement through the weakness of this faithful servant to find Christ's strength in their own weakness. We are better able to know and love each other when we are real, not impressive.

READ JAMES 5:16. What is the intended outcome of sharing our sin and weaknesses with others in the church? Why should there be no shame in sharing our weaknesses among believers in Christ?

Ben asked, "Would you have the courage to begin to share with others where you are desperately in need of prayer?" Would you have the courage to do that now?

CLOSE IN PRAYER

Where I Am

Our shared life together in Christ makes us a family. No one quite knows us like the people who see us at our best and at our worst and still call us their own. In this family, we discover what it means to be fully known and truly loved. In this week's study, we'll see how the experience of being seen, known, and loved should translate to life in the local church.

Consider and respond to the prompts below in light of this question: "Can I be known and loved in the church?"

The view I inherited:

How my view has changed over time:

Factors that have shaped my view:

Reasons I have sometimes been discouraged:

Questions I have:

Search me, God, and know my heart;
test me and know my concerns.
See if there is any offensive way in me;
lead me in the everlasting way.
PSALM 139:23-24

What Scripture Teaches

Name three "must-have" qualities you would want to know are present in a physician you would see about a potentially serious medical condition.

Name three qualities you would want in the pastor of a church you join.

Name three qualities you would want in a friend as you walk through a difficult circumstance.

The answers you gave may not be exactly the same for each scenario, but they likely overlap in important ways. A doctor who doesn't shoot straight isn't worth the smallest copay. A pastor who never acknowledges his own struggles makes overcoming yours seem impossible. A "friend" who doesn't hold space with you in confidence makes you think it's best to handle struggles on your own.

Modern language has given us many words and phrases to describe sincerity—authentic, genuine, true, the realest, legit, one hundred percent. And isn't that what we all want? People we can be real with and who are real with us. You don't always know when you're in that type of a relationship, but Scripture holds it up as the model for the church.

Every day they devoted themselves to meeting together
in the temple, and broke bread from house to house.
They ate their food with joyful and sincere hearts.
ACTS 2:46

READ ACTS 2:37-47, paying special attention to verse 38. What confidence did these members of the first church have to relate to one another with absolute sincerity?

Even in the local church, many of us believe our relationships with other people are contingent upon keeping our worst parts hidden. We want to be fully known and truly loved, but we believe relating that way is too personal, too vulnerable, too risky. If other people really knew us, we would feel uncomfortably exposed, and for good reason—our carefully curated reputations would crash loudly to the floor in the center of the room where God's people are gathered, just trying to have a good time. We imagine our real selves would then be politely excused from the room.

So we must unpack whatever baggage we've carried to make us think in such fearfully cautious terms and start over, allowing our relationship with God to be the foundation of our relationships with each other. That is, after all, how the earliest believers began relating to one another with sincere hearts: They understood their shared responsibility in Christ's death and that they'd all been forgiven by Him (Acts 2:37-38).

READ 1 CORINTHIANS 13:8-13. What seemingly contrary realities does verse 8 indicate about relationship with the Lord?

Our lack of full knowledge about God's love for us
this side of heaven makes that love no less real.

Love never ends. Ongoing revelation (prophecy) will one day end, but love will always remain. God is under no illusions about who you are. He knows your doubts, struggles, heartache, and questions—and He loves you. This is not a one-time truth you receive at salvation and then lose bit by bit with every unsanctified moment going forward. God's love for you never ends. And because He loves you like that, He gives those difficult earthly realities good and holy purpose.

READ 2 CORINTHIANS 12:7-10. How did Paul relate to the Lord in sincerity? Why did God allow Paul's thorn in the flesh to remain?

Not once, not twice, but three times, Paul begged God to make this thing go away! He didn't have to wait long for his answer, though. The Lord answered his prayer quickly. God said, "No," to the instant removal of the thorn, saying the pain was profitable. The thorn was the best medicine for the pride that would have accompanied the unusual knowledge God had given Paul. In the hands of God, a pained Paul was more useful than a puffed-up Paul.

What "thorn in the flesh" do you have? In other words, what physical, mental, emotional, or relational difficulty regularly challenges or humbles you?

Name a few truths about God that you know you can count on in that trial. For help, read Psalm 23:4; Proverbs 3:5-6; Isaiah 43:2; Matthew 11:28-29; Romans 8:28.

Every weakness needs to be taken to God and traded in for the strength only He provides.

The things that caused Paul pain were constantly pushing him back to the throne of grace, which is the only ground for confidence any of us ever has. He didn't try to hide his feelings about his weakness; he acknowledged it as personal torment. Paul was a model for expressing need for Christ and struggle with sin and pain.

What power there is in accepted sorrow! Perhaps we would grow in sincerity with one another if we offered prayers of acceptance:

> *Lord, I accept this season of tension with my spouse and know*
> *You will use it for good.*

> *Lord, I accept this unforeseen illness and know it will force me*
> *to rely on You.*

> *Lord, I accept the death of my dad, as it reminds me every*
> *day of the brevity of my own life.*

> *Lord, I accept the burden and stress of this job, knowing You have*
> *called me to this, that You will equip me for this.*

Consider again the "thorn in the flesh" you identified on the previous page. Prayerfully complete your own sentence of acceptance in the style of the examples given, based on one of the biblical promises you can know as truth.

> *Lord, I accept*

Share this thorn with another believer so they might help bear your burdens (Galatians 6:2).

The sincerity with which we can safely relate to God should inform our relationships with other believers. Because we are fully known and truly loved by Christ, we can be fully known and truly loved within His body, the church.

> *We love because he first loved us.*
> **1 JOHN 4:19**

What Scripture Teaches

What is your greatest strength? What is your biggest weakness? When preparing for an interview, we know to prepare our answers for those two questions. And though we may have difficulty choosing the right words to express those answers, the fact is, we know what they are. Life has taught us. We want others to focus on whatever qualities make us seem impressive, and we want them to overlook anything that might cause them to view us differently. In light of this reality, let's jump into today's personal study with some honest admissions.

In terms of the life of faith, what is your greatest strength?

What do you consider to be your greatest weakness in the life of faith?

The early Christians did not try to impress one another (Acts 2:44-46). They lived their lives out in the open, with nothing to hide. But the temptation to be impressive to other believers is always there, isn't it? Let's think about that word for a moment—*impressive*.

As human beings, we want that word associated with our names. *Have you met so-and-so? That guy is impressive. Have you met her? She is so impressive.*

Who doesn't want to be impressive? To be impressive means we evoke admiration in others. And admiration stokes the fires of our self-worth. It makes us feel exalted and superhuman, like we're on a higher level than other people.

READ 2 CORINTHIANS 10:10. How did the apostle Paul describe himself?

According to his own words, the apostle Paul was not impressive. He did not consider himself better or stronger than other Christians. And his peers had very little confidence in his eloquence and charisma. The description of Paul in this passage is not what most of us would look for in a preacher.

The point is, by the world's standards, one of the most impactful Christ-followers in the New Testament was *weak*. But what the world would consider Paul's weaknesses meant strength in Christ, and he knew it—to the point that he believed it was reason to celebrate among other Christians.

> *But he said to me, "My grace is sufficient for you, for my power is perfected in weakness." Therefore, I will most gladly boast all the more about my weaknesses, so that Christ's power may reside in me. So I take pleasure in weaknesses, insults, hardships, persecutions, and in difficulties, for the sake of Christ. For when I am weak, then I am strong.*
> **2 CORINTHIANS 12:9-10**

Think about Paul's words here in the context of a small group in the local church. What might Paul have named as his prayer request? His praise? How is that similar or different from the type of sharing of life among believers that you've experienced?

Why should we talk honestly about our weaknesses?

As Paul "boasted," or shared his struggle, with others, they developed relational intimacy.

In what ways does pride keep us from fully knowing and truly loving others in the body of Christ?

We learned in this week's first personal study that the early church gathered together with sincerity. As they shared meals, studied Scripture, and prayed together, they did so in authentic humility. And so should the church today. When we gather together, our sense of community will grow as we confess where we are weak, resentful, disobedient, or angry at life's circumstances. All of these things are a normal part of living in the flesh while we wait for heaven. Hiding them doesn't change that. When humbly acknowledged, God will demonstrate our weaknesses as strength. Suffering well causes other people to see Christ in you.

When have you seen humility in weakness positively impact relationships among believers?

READ PHILIPPIANS 2:3. Why does considering others as more important than yourself impact your willingness to admit your struggles to them?

The early church ate together with joyful and sincere hearts (Acts 2:46), but that doesn't mean their lives were nothing but sunshine and roses. They humbly shared their hurts, struggles, and failures. Their willingness to do so increased the power of their witness, and it deepened their connection with one another.

What scares you about humbly acknowledging your weakness to other believers?

What encourages you about engaging with God's people with that kind of honesty?

In order for your connection with others to grow, you must reach that place where you truly open up about your life—the parts you're most proud of and the parts you've been ashamed of.

Whatever it takes, God wants to give you a compassionate servant's heart for people. He wants to help you reach the place where other people are more important than your obsession with personal development. The more pride seeps into your life, the more your view of yourself is elevated and the less effective you will be in serving others and connecting with them in joyful sincerity.

Therefore, confess your sins to one another and pray for one another, so that you may be healed. The prayer of a righteous person is very powerful in its effect.
JAMES 5:16

Where I'm Going

You don't need to have a certain personality type to relate to other people in sincerity. God wants all of His children to experience authentic community together. We can't be fully known and truly loved in the body of Christ if we do not come together in sincerity. But John says in 1 John 1:7, "If we walk in the light as he himself is in the light, we have fellowship with one another, and the blood of Jesus his Son cleanses us from all sin."

So challenge yourself to a deeper level of vulnerability with those around you. It takes courage to be honest, but give yourself permission to be an open book today. Share what you're going through with another believer.

I will most gladly boast all the more about my weaknesses . . .
2 CORINTHIANS 12:9B

One thorn in my flesh, a chronic pain I'm experiencing, is . . .

(This can be physical, emotional, mental, relational, etc.)

. . . so that Christ's power may reside in me.
2 CORINTHIANS 12:9C

One painful moment in my life that God has used for good is . . .

Briefly summarize what happened and a lesson God taught you as a result.

Think of one person with whom you can sincerely and humbly share the circumstances you've described. Reach out to that person and get together to share. Then, use the space below to note what you gain from that conversation.

A little leaven leavens the whole batch of dough.
GALATIANS 5:9

LIVING

GENEROUSLY

TRUTH

The most important
investments we make
are in people.

GROUP STUDY

START

Welcome to session 4 of Together, *"Living Generously."*
Before you dive into the group study, take a few moments to review session 3.

In last week's personal study, we discovered that relating in realness, with sincerity of heart—not trying to be impressive but acknowledging weakness—enables us to be known and loved in the community of faith.

> What did you learn about being known and loved members of God's family, together with other believers, in your study of Acts 2:37-47 and 2 Corinthians 12:9-10?

> Name one step God is leading you to take to relate to other believers with greater sincerity in the days ahead.

The most important investments we make are in people.

We defined sincerity as not trying to be impressive. Another aspect of sincerity, though, is seen in our giving—yes, the giving of our real selves, but also the giving of our time and resources. There is a connection in sincere family relationships where we are known and loved that produces generosity.

In the past few weeks, what are some ways you've learned you need to more generously invest yourself in other believers' lives?

To prepare for the video teaching, pray together and ask God to help each person understand and apply this truth.

WATCH

*Use these statements to follow along as you watch the video teaching
for session 4, and use the blank space to take additional notes.*

In the context of relating generously within the community of faith, there are three
main areas of life to which we should give attention:

    1. The highs

    2. The lows

    3. The transitions

ROMANS 12:15

When you use your money to build relationships, there will be people in heaven to
receive you one day because you invested in people, not in things that pass away.

LUKE 16:1-15

Develop eyes to see the people that God has put around you, and look for intentional
ways to be there for them.

ACTS 2:45

To access the video teaching sessions,
use the instructions in the back
of your Bible study book.

GROUP STUDY

DISCUSS

Use these questions and prompts to discuss the video teaching.

What stood out to you personally in Ben's teaching?

How would you define relational generosity? Should that be an expectation we have in the community of faith? Why?

Ben noted that some of us are better at financial generosity than relational generosity, and vice versa. But we don't have to choose one over the other. We shouldn't choose one over the other! Both financial and relational generosity were prioritized in the early church, and all of it mattered.

READ ACTS 2:42-47. Name examples of financial generosity seen in the passage. Name examples of relational generosity.

Now, name an example of generous living you've seen or experienced in the community of faith. How did that generosity impact togetherness among believers?

Which is the greater challenge for you, financial or relational generosity? Why?

We need to aim to live generously as church family in three contexts: the highs, the lows, and the transitions. Let's talk about each of those in practical terms. In Romans 12:15, Paul wrote, "Rejoice with those who rejoice; weep with those who weep."

Think about Paul's words in Romans 12:15 in terms of the highs and the lows of life. What would it look like for you to rejoice with another believer who is rejoicing? Give an example.

Of the two instructions Paul gives in Romans 12:15, rejoicing with those who rejoice sounds easiest. However, many times, rejoicing doesn't feel easy or natural.

Why might rejoicing with those who rejoice sometimes feel like an act of sacrificial generosity?

What would it look like for you to weep with another believer who is weeping? Can you live out the heart of this without actually shedding tears? Give an example of a way we can relate generously to other believers in the lows.

How can you relate generously to another believer who is going through a transition in life?

Jesus used a strange story about a dishonest manager to teach us about relational generosity. You'll dig deeper into that story in your personal study this week, but let's read it now, along with another verse Ben mentioned, so that we might head into our study with the right framework and intention.

READ LUKE 16:1-15 AND PSALM 90:12. What is God already teaching you about togetherness in the body of Christ in this session on living generously?

CLOSE IN PRAYER

Where I Am

Were you stretched outside your comfort zone in last week's study? The sincerity of faith shared by the early church in Acts 2 certainly has the potential to challenge sensibilities about relating to others. We shouldn't stop there or go backwards, though. Sincerity of faith is a starting point, not an end. As we step into God's vision as a family that knows and loves each other, we'll invest in one another generously in various ways.

Consider and respond to the prompts below in light of this question: "What is my role in the church family?"

The view I inherited:

How my view has changed over time:

Factors that have shaped my view:

Reasons I have sometimes been discouraged:

Questions I have:

Search me, God, and know my heart;
test me and know my concerns.
See if there is any offensive way in me;
lead me in the everlasting way.
PSALM 139:23-24

What Scripture Teaches

In what circumstances or relationships would you consider yourself generous? In what way(s) are you generous in those situations or with those people? Why?

Now, think about a relationship or life context in which you are not generous. Why is it difficult for you to be generous with that person or in that situation?

READ AGAIN ACTS 2:42-47. What kind of generosity existed among the believers in the early church?

Now all the believers were together and held all things in common. They sold their possessions and property and distributed the proceeds to all, as any had need.
ACTS 2:44-45

What reasons might the earliest believers have had for giving to one another so extravagantly?

Unusual generosity marked the early church. The believers in Acts invested in one another. They shared financially as they had need, and they also prioritized time to do life together and to minister to each other.

They were *together.*
They held *everything in common.*
They readily *met each others' needs.*

And it made sense. Jesus had taught them to live with a kingdom mindset. After He died on the cross, rose from the dead, and ascended before their eyes into heaven, they had a better understanding of what that kind of mindset entailed.

> *"Don't store up for yourselves treasures on earth, where moth*
> *and rust destroy and where thieves break in and steal.*
> *But store up for yourselves treasures in heaven, where neither moth*
> *nor rust destroys, and where thieves don't break in and steal.*
> *For where your treasure is, there your heart will be also."*
> **MATTHEW 6:19-21**

Restate Jesus's teaching in your own words.

Giving is more about the posture of our hearts than a set amount. The early church modeled a kind of generous living that proved their hearts were untethered to earthly treasures. They knew their stuff would one day disappear, so instead of accumulating temporary possessions that only have limited value, they set their hearts on eternal life with Jesus and robust relationships with other believers.

Believers in the local church should strive for a strong
sense of connectedness. Those relationships built on earth
will have eternal value, unlike most things we collect.

Jesus nails this subject on the head in the strangest parable ever spoken. It's about a dirty, rotten manager who woke up one day to a harsh reality. His career was coming to a crashing halt, and he had nowhere to turn. He had to come up with a plan quick.

READ LUKE 16:1-10. Why did the manager hatch this plan (v. 4)?

Did Jesus really use a dishonest man to illustrate spiritual truth and wisdom? He did. Think about it this way—every single one of us is a mixed bag of beauty and brokenness. Under that lens, the story about a dishonest manager is entirely relatable. And it has good purpose. Jesus's point isn't about cheating, bribery, or flattery. He praised the very flawed manager for having the foresight to see beyond the present moment and build relationships.

How would your use of and attitude about money change if you looked past your present circumstances and focused on eternity?

Look back at your answer to the question at the bottom of page 72. How does this parable help you better understand why the early church generously invested in one another?

Like the dishonest manager, and like the Christians in Acts 2, we need to look past today. Accumulating money is not our goal in life. God wants us to use our finances to prepare us for the life to come. In other words, live today as if you're going to lose everything you own tomorrow. Live your life today as if the only thing that's going to be left next week is your relationships.

What are some specific ways we can embrace and embody the lesson Jesus teaches in this parable?

Jesus's message in Luke 16:1-10 shocks us, and rightly so. It should shock us to know that many non-Christians often show greater wisdom in long-range planning than most Christians. The dishonest manager thought about the future as he handled money, and Jesus praised him as the hero of the story. Flawed as he was, he leveraged relationships and considered where he was going to wind up one day.

Building people is better than building capital. Part of what Jesus is teaching is, "Invest your money in your friendships so that when your money is gone, these individuals will welcome you into eternal dwellings." If we minimize relationships, we do so to our own detriment.

Wise people think about eternal realities now, not later.

A WORD ON TITHING

As we will see in the next personal study, biblical generosity isn't only about money. But, to be clear, money is certainly a part of it. Money is a big deal to Jesus—He talked more about money than prayer! Money is one indicator of how much hold the world has on us. When we are distressed about parting with money or possessions, that's a sure sign we're valuing treasures on earth over treasures in heaven.

If you're part of the large number of churchgoers who tip rather than tithe, you need to know that isn't the biblical model for generosity and sharing. The word *tithe* means ten percent. God calls us to practice faithful 10% giving as a baseline. If we aren't obedient in this, we are failing one of His tests on our character, which could cause a major disruption of His favor in our lives (Malachi 3:8-12).

What Scripture Teaches

Living in light of eternity, where our treasure rests in heaven, frees us to live differently. Our attitude towards our needs and our possessions is no longer earth-bound. We're able to see our needs and the needs of others in a different light. Rather than hording stuff and amassing wealth that is temporary, we can leverage what God has given us toward heaven-focused generosity.

Note what each of the following verses teaches about generosity.

Acts 3:1-11.

Luke 6:30.

Psalm 37:21.

Hebrews 13:16.

2 Corinthians 8:1-7

Throughout God's Word, we find both examples and exhortations that compel us to live generously. In fact, generosity is actually the way we store up treasures in heaven. When Peter and John encountered the lame man outside the temple, they responded to him generously. They did not have money to offer, but they gave the most valuable treasure they had—Christ's power for physical and spiritual healing (Acts 3:1-10). In other passages, Scripture teaches us to love people, not possessions—even if those people take advantage of us. God is pleased with a lifestyle of sacrificial generosity, where His people go above and beyond to diligently love others in every way.

Worldly wealth won't last, so invest yourself in people.

It's so easy to get caught up in busyness and just go through the motions! Investing yourself in people takes intentionality. What does it look like to generously invest yourself in people? Let's consider three key moments in life that allow you to invest generously in others with sacrificial love.

THE HIGHS

Rejoice with those who rejoice.
ROMANS 12:15A

Think of one of your most celebratory moments. Who in your life genuinely celebrated with you? Why?

Has there ever been a time when others did not celebrate an important moment with you? Why?

Why is it sometimes difficult for us to rejoice with those who rejoice?

It's a strange, isolating feeling to experience something special with nobody there to celebrate with you. Sometimes, this happens because we don't tell others about the special moment for fear of seeming prideful or braggadocious. Other times, people distance themselves from our happy outcomes because of their own human tendency to compare and envy. And God wants us to take Paul's words in Romans 12 to heart. We invest generously in other people by genuinely and generously celebrating them.

Who do you know that is experiencing great joy? What could you do to let that person know you're rejoicing with them?

THE LOWS

Weep with those who weep.
ROMANS 12:15B

Have you ever faced a difficult situation without a strong friendship to lean on through that circumstance? If so, how did you feel? If not, how have your friendships supported you through hardships?

Heaven will be a place with no more tears, but here on earth, there are plenty. In this broken world, despair, grief, and sorrow break our hearts and rend our tears.

In Matthew 26:36-46, Jesus asked His closest friends to stay alert, pray, and be near to Him in His time of testing. Sadly, they all fell asleep instead.

What are some signs we might have "fallen asleep" in our relationships with people who are facing hard times?

In the darkest night of His soul, Jesus wanted His loved ones close. All of us want that kind of support when we face difficult circumstances. And most of us know multiple people walking through fierce trials—cancer, the loss of a relative, the sting of defeat in closing a business, the loss of a dream, etc.

As you think about these people, jot down their names, and pray about ways you might generously invest in them during their time of trouble.

THE TRANSITIONS

*And let us consider one another in order
to provoke love and good works.*
HEBREWS 10:24

Name a season of transition you've experienced. Were there people who helped you make that transition well? If so, how? If not, why?

Life is full of highs, lows, and transitions. Of the three categories, transitions tend to be ignored the most. But in the big changes of life, people need extra love and support.

Make a list of people you know who are moving into new seasons of life, and consider how you can come alongside them and help them feel less alone.

You might wonder, "What do I have to give generously to others?" The answer to that question is about more than money or possessions. The biggest thing you have to give others is an outward expression of your faith—a sacrificial sharing of who you are in Christ. And you do that when you invest yourself in loving relationships with other people—rejoicing, weeping, and coming alongside to support them in any and every circumstance life brings.

Where I'm Going

If we want to follow Jesus's teachings, which include the parable of the dishonest manager, we must apply them to our lives in practical ways. Jesus didn't hold people at arm's length—He invited them to come to Him so that He might embrace them wholly. What about you? Are you making a difference in other people's lives? Who are the people who know you care about them—in the good, the bad, and the ugly? Are you willing to relate in that way to other believers in the local church?

Thoughtfully consider the following questions, and ask God to open your heart and help you be willing to relationally invest with other believers.

How can we generously share our concern for others through prayer?

In what relationships are you intentionally leaning in and getting to know the other person more and more each week? Who are you letting in so they can get to know you? What do you need to do so that kind of transparency can happen?

What younger person in your life could you invest in? What specific way could you support the next generation and be for someone else what you needed when you were young?

Surely you can think of a moment in your life when you needed someone and felt all alone. Conversely, you may recall a time when someone in your life needed you and you just weren't there. This is where the real essence of Christianity shines brightest. Jesus died for all those moments when we or others have fallen short.

How are you reaching out to others who are experiencing the same hurts you've experienced?

In what relationships have you not been intentional to invest yourself through care and concern? What is God leading you to do in those relationships now?

A little leaven leavens the whole batch of dough.
GALATIANS 5:9

SESSION 5

REACHING

BEYOND

TRUTH

Community is
designed to expand.

GROUP STUDY

START

Welcome to session 5 of Together, *"Reaching Beyond."*
Before you dive into the group study, take a few moments to review session 4.

Let's revisit what we learned in last week's study on living generously. We were reminded that the most important investments we make are the investments we make in people. In fact, our togetherness in the local church depends on it! You can't go deep with people to whom you don't give any time or attention.

> What did you learn about the value of relational generosity in your study of Acts 2:37-47, Romans 12:15, and Luke 16:1-15?

> Name one step God is leading you to take to generously invest in other believers in the days ahead.

As individual believers, we understand that our obedience is a witness to other people. That is certainly true about togetherness in the community of faith! As we see God's vision for the church, relate with one another sincerely—being known and loved as family—and live generously, God will use our togetherness to draw other people to Himself and into the church.

Community is designed to expand.

Which describes the way you feel about growth in your local church, especially in your own small group: expectant and excited or uncomfortable and anxious?

— *To prepare for the video teaching, pray together and ask God to help each person understand and apply this truth.*

WATCH

Use these statements to follow along as you watch the video teaching for session 5, and use the blank space to take additional notes.

A healthy church is a growing church where people are compelled to reach outside the walls.

ACTS 2:47

Invite people into your life, not to a location.

MARK 2:13-17

Five observations in Mark 2 that teach us how to interact with the nonreligious:

    1. Jesus saw Levi, making eye contact with him.

    2. Jesus invited Levi to follow Him, and Levi did.

    3. Levi invited his nonreligious friends over for dinner with Jesus.

    4. Jesus was judged for eating with sinners.

    5. Jesus lived by His primary mission—to seek and save the lost.

To access the video teaching sessions, use the instructions in the back of your Bible study book.

GROUP STUDY

DISCUSS

Use these questions and prompts to discuss the video teaching.

What stood out to you personally in Ben's teaching?

Ben said, "Community is designed to expand." Do you think your church lives with that expectation? Explain your answer.

Whose responsibility does our communal behavior show we believe the task of "reaching beyond" to be (e.g., church leaders, staff, the congregation)?

Churches often spend much more time talking about reaching beyond the walls of the church than they do actually reaching beyond those walls. Evangelism is an understood New Testament directive, yet that directive is often met with uncertainty, fear, and misunderstanding. We know Jesus wants us to reach beyond, but our inclination is to stay focused within.

READ MARK 2:13-17, and review the five observations Ben made. What in this list is especially instructive to you today?

How can we implement these five concepts into local church life, especially small groups within the local church, as a way to reach beyond?

We might wish Mark had filled in some blanks between verses 14 and 15. Is it surprising to you that Levi answered Jesus's call to follow Him and also continued in relationship with sinful people?

Ben said, "The most effective evangelism we do is in the context of trusted relationships," and, "Hospitality is one of the greatest ways to win people to Christ."

Respond to these two statements. How do these truths challenge you personally? How should they impact our understanding and practice of togetherness?

Our togetherness involves reaching beyond ourselves to invite others in—and that's hard. So Ben named some ways we can build the expectation for and anticipation of reaching beyond our group in gospel conversations with people outside the church. He said, "Have a time when you share stories of gospel conversations where the Lord opened up a door for you to go deeper in sharing your own faith story with somebody . . . Find a place in the city where you can serve together . . . Have times where you debrief what you learned or consider how you might take the next step in forming relationships through those contexts."

What are some other ways we can encourage each other to reach beyond?

Ben said, "We gather so that we can scatter." What does that mean?

Who do you know that doesn't know Christ? What can you do about it?

CLOSE IN PRAYER

Where I Am

When the body of Christ functions in a healthy way, we can be tempted to drift into what you may have heard referred to as a "holy huddle." Seeing God's vision and living generously together as a family that knows and loves each other is comfortable and affirming. It can be incredibly fun, too. But this comfort often tempts us to settle our gaze inwardly, ignoring Christ's command that we invite people who stand outside those glorious realities to come in.

Consider and respond to the prompts below in light of this question: "How do we relate to people outside the church?"

The view I inherited:

How my view has changed over time:

Factors that have shaped my view:

Reasons I have sometimes been discouraged:

Questions I have:

Search me, God, and know my heart;
test me and know my concerns.
See if there is any offensive way in me;
lead me in the everlasting way.
PSALM 139:23-24

What Scripture Teaches

Do you think every person in the body of Christ should have a heart and passion to reach new people for Jesus? Explain your answer.

Every day the Lord added to their number those who were being saved.
ACTS 2:47B

Can you even imagine it? What would it be like if your local church saw someone come to faith in Christ every single day this year? What a revival it would create to witness lives being transformed by the gospel—*daily*.

Yet according to recent research, 94% of churchgoers claim they attended church as a child.[1] That means only 6% of people in our churches are coming for the first time as adults. We have a lot of work to do to bring those who were raised outside of Christian households into the church.

Even if we all agree that every believer should have a heart and passion to reach new people for Jesus, most Christians aren't engaging with people according to that belief. This reality should make us wonder why, and it should cause us to examine ourselves.

REREAD ACTS 2:42-47. What about the early church lets us know its members shared a heartfelt passion to reach new people for Jesus?

What about your local church lets people know its members share a heartfelt passion to reach new people for Jesus?

---

1. Earls, Aaron. "Most Protestant Churchgoers Don't Go to Church Alone." Lifeway Research. Lifeway Christian Resources, February 25, 2020. https://research.lifeway.com/2020/02/25/most-protestant-churchgoers-dont-go-to-church-alone/.

What about your church might lead people to think that its members don't have a passion for the lost?

Two things on earth will go beyond the grave:
the words of God and the souls of people.

Over and over again, the Bible reminds us of the brevity of life and the call to invest in eternal things (Psalm 49:16-17). It also shows us through the example of the early church that being missionally focused is a natural outcome of living together in Christ (Acts 2:47).

When believers together devote themselves to learning from God's Word, caring and sharing, choosing to forgive, and praying, they'll understand what matters most and live by that understanding. As they do, they'll stand out as altogether different from the world. God will draw people to Himself through the beautiful realities their faithful community proves.

READ MARK 2:13-17. What similarities can you see between this account and the account of the early church in Acts 2:42-47?

Because of Levi's occupation, we know that he was a hated man. He ran a toll booth that was positioned along the road. He searched people's bags and charged them fees for income taxes, sales taxes, and even toll taxes. Men in Levi's position were notorious for rounding up the rate and taking advantage of people. Most of the Jews had written Levi off, but there was one Jew who had not—Jesus.

What does Jesus's invitation, "Follow me" (v. 14), teach you about what Jesus saw in Levi as he sat at the tax collector's booth?

Jesus *saw* Levi, and that simple truth is instructive for the church today. You never know which people around you are ready for a change. Maybe you won't be able to tell at first glance—you have to really look in order to see them.

Are there people who keep popping up in your life? A barista at the coffee shop, an employee at your favorite book store, a parent at the soccer field? God brings people into your life for a purpose, and He wants you to develop eyes to see them.

Evangelism starts with seeing people right in front
of you whom others have chosen to ignore.

How did Levi respond to Jesus's invitation (vv. 14-15)? In his new life with Christ, why would Levi invite his sinful friends and coworkers over for dinner with Jesus?

In a single moment, Levi got up and followed Jesus. And then, he started inviting other people to follow Jesus, too. Because Levi remained in relationship with nonreligious folks, he was in a prime position to expose them to Jesus. He invited them over for dinner so they could know the One who was changing him.

When is the last time you had unbelievers over for dinner?

*Evangelism is not something assigned to the few brave folks
in the congregation. It is a call on every Christian's life.*

REREAD MARK 2:13-17. Who had embraced the temptation to create a
"holy huddle" to exclude outsiders and were sticking to it? Why?

What dangers are there for a local church body that isn't unified together
in Jesus's call to embrace sinners and share the gospel with them?

Religious people judged Jesus for eating with sinners. They probably blasted Him with
proof texts like Proverbs 13:20b, "A companion of fools will suffer harm." They wondered,
"Doesn't this Jesus guy read the Old Testament? Doesn't He know that we religious people
create holy huddles and we stay inside them? We don't go where sinners go. That's how
holiness works." But Jesus had a different strategy.

> *When Jesus heard this, he told them, "It is not those
> who are well who need a doctor, but those who are sick.
> I didn't come to call the righteous, but sinners."*
> **MARK 2:17**

The focus of Jesus's life was those who were far off. Call them the unbelieving, uncouth,
unchurched, unsaved—whatever "un" you prefer. The Lord had His eyes on people who
felt no need for religion. Will you?

*Evangelism carries out Jesus's mission to fill
up heaven with sinners saved by grace.*

What Scripture Teaches

Start today's study by taking a look back at the last paragraph and statement on the previous page. A question was left hanging over us with no direct instruction to respond, and that was by design. Pondering our commitment to Christ helps us embrace deeper realities in Christ.

> *Do not be conformed to this age, but be transformed by the renewing of your mind, so that you may discern what is the good, pleasing, and perfect will of God.*
> **ROMANS 12:2**

Have you ever heard a sermon on Jesus's Great Commission in Matthew 28:18-20? What about Jesus's promise in Acts 1:8, that we will receive the Spirit's power to be His witnesses in our own hometowns and all around the world? These texts are commonly used to stir the community of faith to evangelism.

If we're hearing and pondering truths about Jesus's mission to reach the lost, why aren't believers everywhere sharing the gospel? Let's not stop at briefly considering heady questions about our part in Jesus's mission. Transformation happens when our minds are renewed by the truths that confront us in God's Word. In other words, thoughtful consideration should be met by honest answers and an openness to change. Only then will we truly examine ourselves in light of Jesus's example.

Is the focus of Jesus's life (filling up heaven with sinners saved by grace) the focus of your life? Is it the focus of your local church?

If so, what about you demonstrates that focus? If not, what's keeping you from embracing that focus?

You may spend the vast majority of your time with Christian people and feel most comfortable with them. You might also feel entirely uncomfortable or ill-equipped to evangelize the lost. But no matter the context of your work and social life, it is impossible for any believer to get away from the thrust of Jesus's mission, which was and is to engage the unchristian.

How do we reach the lost? We've got to get to know them.

READ 1 CORINTHIANS 16:13-14. Note the five commands given here. What connection is there between each command and getting to know lost people?

Be alert.

Stand firm in faith.

Be courageous.

Be strong.

Do everything in love.

Genuine friendship is our greatest path to evangelism. What makes you appealing to a nonreligious person is not your religion, it's the relationship you offer them. And that can only develop if you're alert to the people around you, courageously engaging in strong relationship, and standing firm in faith with each conversation you have—with love as your motive for all of it. Nonreligious people think most of what we Christians do is weird, but love is never off-putting.

Which of the following are difficult for you: being alert every day to the people God places in your life, engaging with unbelievers in meaningful relationship, standing firm in faith in every conversation you have, or relating to people in the love of Christ? Why?

What can you do to . . .

be more alert to the people around you?

engage with unbelievers in meaningful relationship?

stand firm in faith in every conversation?

relate to others in the love of Christ?

Nonreligious people will listen once they feel loved.

Most unbelievers think that all Christians are judgmental. We are perceived as always looking down our noses at their parties, their weekend activities, their purchases, their *lives*. We are perceived as enemies. It doesn't have to be that way. Spending quality time in true friendship with nonreligious people is the best way to help them see the grace and goodness of Jesus.

When have you earned the trust of an unbeliever through friendship? How did that happen?

The wounds of a friend can be trusted,
but an enemy multiplies kisses.
PROVERBS 27:6 NIV

Or do you despise the riches of his kindness, restraint,
and patience, not recognizing that God's kindness
is intended to lead you to repentance?
ROMANS 2:4

Some might object and argue, "Hanging out with people doesn't get them into heaven! You have to confront them with the gospel, and the gospel is offensive." How do Proverbs 26:5-6 and Romans 2:4 challenge that posture?

Sharing the message of Christ is absolutely essential for seeing lives changed, and friendship opens the door for gospel conversations like nothing else. You can't rush evangelism. It takes time. Will you invest in the lives of nonreligious people? Will you love them well? Remember, it is God's kindness that leads them to repentance, and God's kindness is meant to be displayed in you.

Where I'm Going

The Lord adding to the number of Christians daily isn't a reality that should remain in the first-century church. He wants every local church to grow in number. In fact, Jesus commands us to continue reaching beyond our circles and bringing others into His family—which happens as we love God and love people (Matthew 22:37-39). That's His plan until the end: "This good news of the kingdom will be proclaimed in all the world as a testimony to all nations, and then the end will come" (Matthew 24:14).

Will your church join Him in reaching beyond? Will you? Here are some specific ways you can live like a missonary in your neighborhood.

Learn the names of your neighbors, including their kids' names. Write them below.

Start praying for those people by name. Write a prayer for them in the space below.

The Bible says we should practice hospitality. *Hospitality* means "to welcome strangers." Who on your street is still a stranger, and what can you do to change that? Name a few ways below (e.g., walk across the street when they're outside and introduce yourself, have them over for a dinner) and commit to taking action on at least one of these ideas this week. Make it fun!

A little leaven leavens the whole batch of dough.
GALATIANS 5:9

SESSION 6

MAINTAINING

UNITY

TRUTH

Community requires that
we keep showing up and
giving each other grace.

GROUP STUDY

START

Welcome everyone to session 6 of Together, *"Maintaining Unity."*
Before you dive into the group study, take a few minutes to review session 5.

Today begins our final session in our study of *Together: Community That Marked the Acts 2 Church.* This week, we'll wrap up by considering the importance of maintaining the gospel unity we've come to understand as critical to our togetherness, no matter what circumstances or relational challenges we face. Before we jump in, let's review last week's study on reaching beyond.

In your study of Acts 2:42-47, Mark 2:13-17, and 1 Corinthians 16:13-14, what did you learn about the mission we share together to reach beyond?

Name one step God is leading you to take to reach beyond the walls of your church in the days ahead.

Community requires that we keep showing up and giving each other grace.

In session 1, we began by taking a look at God's vision for the church—*togetherness*—which Jesus prayed about in John 17:21 and the early church lived out in Acts 2. Since then, we've learned His vision grows within us and shows up relationally as we devote ourselves to it. That's an ongoing reality. God wants us to know and experience togetherness longer than these six weeks—and it requires intentionality and commitment.

When relationships get hard, are you more likely to walk away or stick it out?

To prepare for the video teaching, pray together and ask God to help each person understand and apply this truth.

WATCH

Use these statements to follow along as you watch the video teaching
for session 6, and use the blank space to take additional notes.

We must hold the main things with the highest importance and not allow the little things to distract us from being together.

ACTS 2:44

Is there a chapter and verse attached to what offends you in community, or is it just an issue of preference?

ROMANS 14

There's a loving way to confront someone, and it should be the norm in the church and not the exception.

PROVERBS 27:5-6

Stay together. Continue to look for ways to give grace and receive it so that the Lord can be glorified as we build His church.

To access the video teaching sessions,
use the instructions in the back
of your Bible study book.

GROUP STUDY

DISCUSS

Use these questions and prompts to discuss the video teaching.

What stood out to you personally in Ben's teaching?

Acts 2:44 says this about the first church: "Now all the believers were together and held all things in common." This doesn't mean everyone agreed on the best worship song, the best way to do small groups, or who brought the best dish to the potluck. As Ben explained, it means they held the main things as most important and didn't let anything distract them from that priority of gospel unity.

How would you describe what "everything in common" would mean in your community of faith?

What are some distractions that tend to get in the way of maintaining that type of unity?

READ ROMANS 14:1-4,19-20. When conflict is present among us, what principle should we live by to maintain unity and togetherness?

Just like you'll never be in close relationship with another person without any conflict, you'll never experience depth of relationships in a church without conflict. And that's okay! Ben said, "Confrontation is not the enemy of intimacy." In fact, the most valuable relationships we have on earth come out of working through confrontation, because when we do that, "there's a cost associated with the relationship that's been paid."

In your experience, has confrontation in relationships been the enemy or ally of intimacy? How so?

READ PROVERBS 27:5-6. Think about your relationships in the body of Christ. What does Proverbs 27:5-6 express as the "better" and "trustworthy" way of relating?

What is hard about that for you?

Think again about what Ben's said: The most valuable relationships we have come from working through confrontation, "because there's a cost associated with the relationship that's been paid." We've named the cost, but what is the value? What benefit is there to "an open reprimand" and "the wounds of a friend" (Proverbs 27:5-6) in the context of church life?

God's Word makes it clear: If there's been a disruption to unity, it's up to us to connect with the person or people involved and try to make it right. Ben encouraged us, "Stay together. Continue to look for ways to give grace and receive it so that the Lord can be glorified as we build His church."

How can we summarize what it takes to maintain unity and togetherness for the long haul?

How has this study encouraged you about the future of your life with others in the church? How has it challenged you?

CLOSE IN PRAYER

Where I Am

In this sixth and final session of *Together*, we'll circle back to where we began. God's vision for the church is that we be unified together in Jesus and the realities of His gospel of grace. That's far easier said than done! Yet God calls us to persevere and devote ourselves to maintaining the unity He gives us in Christ. We each bring varied human experiences with us through the church doors, and conflict is inevitable. Maintaining unity, then, involves identifying the messaging and expectations we have learned throughout our lives so we can invite God to align our minds and hearts with the mind and heart of His Spirit in us.

Consider and respond to the prompts below in light of this question: "How do we persevere as a church when it's hard or messy?"

The view I inherited:

How my view has changed over time:

Factors that have shaped my view:

Reasons I have sometimes been discouraged:

Questions I have:

Search me, God, and know my heart;
test me and know my concerns.
See if there is any offensive way in me;
lead me in the everlasting way.
PSALM 139:23-24

What Scripture Teaches

Have you ever looked at your local church in comparison to other churches you could attend? Why are we tempted toward comparison? Why does the proverbial church lawn grass sometimes look greener on the other side?

No church is perfect, but some believers spend their lives seeking out the closest thing. Even if you've been a member of the same church for 40 years, you get it. You love it, but there are things you'd change if you had the chance. We all want our churches to do better, in whatever ways we know to define that.

An up-close study of the very first church might compound that frustration in us a bit. We might read about the first church and feel like our relationships and church culture just don't measure up. The reality in the passage we've been studying in Acts 2 wasn't short-lived, either. The first years in the life of the church contained confrontations, threats, beatings, arrests, imprisonments, and even the martyrdom of Christians. Yet the church continued to grow numerically and in unity together.

READ ACTS 4:1-4,32-35. How do the positive outcomes of growth and unity in these circumstances strike you—common or uncommon in the church today? Relatable or unrelatable? Expected or unexpected? Why?

Now the entire group of those who believed were of one heart and mind, and no one claimed that any of his possessions was his own, but instead they held everything in common.
ACTS 4:32

Because the doctrine of depravity is so clearly described in Scripture, Acts 4:32 and any other verse that describes the exemplary nature of the early church cannot possibly mean that their relationships were rosy, heavenly, and perfect. What Luke described in that early community was peaceful unity, not complete agreement on every issue and matter.

If the early church's grass was greener than ours, it's because these baby Christians understood unity as essential. They took action to build and protect it. Later, Paul would challenge the believers to seek the Holy Spirit's help in keeping relationships warm.

> *Make every effort to keep the unity of the*
> *Spirit through the bond of peace.*
> **EPHESIANS 4:3 NIV**

Why might Paul need to instruct people who once treasured unity as essential to now make the effort to maintain it?

The reality of our fallen nature not only affects us as individuals but as families, too. And that is what the church is—together, we are God's family. In that family, we will disagree at times. Conflict will arise. We will occasionally feel unappreciated, unseen, and even unloved—maybe to the point that we might want to disengage from the church body altogether. So we can't end our study without a look at the importance of relational healing in the body of Christ.

In healthy church families, there is a commitment to
stay together through the thick and thin of life.

Reread the sentence at the bottom of the last page. Now, respond with two sentences of your own that push back against it, and begin like this:

But what if . . .

But what about . . .

We can all reason our way around the essential nature of unity in the church. If we've engaged in relationships in any church for very long, we know from experience that some churches continue for decades in an unhealthy, disunified way. But God knew that when His Spirit directed Paul to pen the words of Ephesians 4:3, and He still wants us to pay attention to its message today.

> **READ ROMANS 14:1-12.** What topics caused disunity among these Christians? Underline the answer in each pair below.
>
> the gospel of grace or what to eat for dinner
>
> the existence of heaven and hell or what days are okay to have parties

Paul identified the two disagreeing groups as weak in faith and strong in faith. Those who were strong understood Christian freedom. They weren't perfect, but they knew that in Christ, they were no longer bound by the law. They didn't feel guilt or shame anymore about eating pork or skipping a traditional holiday.

The weaker group wasn't ready to let go of their traditions. They had grown up with rules, and those rules were not easily abandoned. They were genuine, committed Christians—every bit as loved by God—but they were living with a constant feeling of guilt about laying aside old laws. So they had strong opinions about issues like food and festivals in the church.

Paul had strong words for both groups. Name every instruction Paul gave one or both groups to do and to *not* do. The first of each is given as an example.

Do This	Don't Do This
welcome anyone who is weak in faith	*argue about nonessential matters*

How does this passage help you know when to speak and when to be silent about matters that might be disputed in the church?

Some things in life are worthy of debate. Some issues should make our blood pump fast and our faces turn red. Most things do not fall in this category, and Christians are constantly tempted to major in the minors—to "sweat the small stuff."

Do you ever do that? Has there ever been a time when you majored in something minor regarding church life? What was it? What did you learn?

In our final study, we'll dig into Romans 14 to find principles for maintaining unity, but first, let's center our hearts and minds on the main point we all need to receive: Sometimes, instead of being together in the type of community that marked the Acts 2 church, we make a big deal out of nothing, create tension, and disrupt the unity Jesus died for us to experience.

Christians must strive to live at peace with one another, even when we disagree.

What Scripture Teaches

How would you answer someone who asks, "Why should we accept people we disagree with in our church? Why should we try to maintain unity instead of realizing there are some people we just can't get along with?"

The disagreement Paul addressed in Romans 14 was about food and festivals. Do you ever argue over trivial things with other believers? Why?

When Paul heard about the petty things causing conflict in the Roman church, he could hardly believe it. So he put down some principles for maintaining unity.

Three reasons we should accept those who disagree with us in our churches:

1. God has accepted them (Romans 14:1-3).

We have begun each week of this study by identifying the baggage we bring to our relationships in the local church.

How has that process aided your learning about togetherness among believers?

The Jews and Gentiles in Rome had some baggage of their own. And God would use all of it to help them understand how Jesus's death and resurrection should impact their togetherness as the church. Jesus fulfilled the law and became the source of righteousness, overcoming any baggage like the rules and customs that had come between Christians in Rome.

READ ROMANS 14:1-3. How is God's acceptance of anyone who is "weak in faith" meant to impact our relationships in the body of Christ?

God has a good attitude toward all Christians who carry all types of baggage. He wasn't angry at Jews who chose to eat carrots and beans, and He wasn't angry at Gentiles who preferred pork chops. God did not, and does not, discriminate according to someone's diet—so we should not discriminate. We should receive people who have different preferences because they are deeply loved by God.

God loves and also likes different kinds of people. He prefers diversity to uniformity. But we like to associate with people who dress like us, eat like us, read what we read, vote how we vote, and recreate like we recreate. We like uniformity, but the body of Christ is not uniform. The church is multi-ethnic, multi-generational, and multi-opinionated for a reason. This diversity represents the power of God to reconcile all people to Himself.

> *Welcome anyone who is weak in faith . . .*
> *because God has accepted him.*
> **ROMANS 14:1A,3C**

What preferences that other believers have get in the way of your unity with them? What can you do to welcome or accept them as God does?

We maintain unity in the church when we accept those God accepts, being generous and gracious in disputable matters.

2. Your opinion of another Christian does not matter to God (Romans 14:4).

Who are you to judge another's household servant?
Before his own Lord he stands or falls. And he will
stand, because the Lord is able to make him stand.
ROMANS 14:4

Does this mean that anything goes? Should we gladly accept the sinful actions of those with whom God has joined us together in Christ? Why?

Remember, Paul was addressing disputable matters among Christians—those things about which Scripture is silent, not black-and-white sin.

READ LUKE 17:3. What are we to do when other Christians sin? What are we not to do when others have opinions we disagree with (Romans 14:4)?

READ JUDE 24. How should this future promise help us maintain unity now?

The believers you disagree with or argue with—both in person and online—will stand before God just as you will. They will give an account for their viewpoint, as will you. And despite both your strong opinions, Jesus will fill the gaps for each of you.

We maintain unity in the church when we stand
together now as we will in heaven—joyfully and
without shame because of the grace of God.

3. Every Christian must live according to his or her own conscience (Romans 14:5-9).

Different people have different convictions, and that won't change this side of glory. Each member of Christ's body should pray about their personal convictions and be settled on them. And once we form those convictions, we should not compromise them or let any other person lead us to compromise.

> *Let each one be fully convinced in his own mind.*
> **ROMANS 14:5C**

The other side of that is equally true: We shouldn't impose our convictions about disputable matters on other Christians. Instead, we must remain gracious toward those who do things differently than we do. Each Christian must live for the Lord, not for the unanimous approval of others.

Give one example of a disputable matter about which you disagree with some in the body of Christ (e.g., the age at which it is right for your child to start dating, working on a Sunday, wearing shorts to church on a Sunday).

What does Romans 14:5-9 lead you to think, say, or do?

We maintain unity in the church when we prayerfully honor our convictions to personally honor God.

Where I'm Going

As we finish this study, we want to challenge you to stick with your church through seasons of agreement and disagreement, particularly when the arguments are about issues outside the gospel. A church that stays together is glorifying to God.

Identify some disagreements that may exist or do exist in your local church context.

Now, evaluate those disagreements based on Romans 14:1-12, using the following criteria:

Is the stance you're taking welcoming of those who are newer in faith?

Is the disagreement over a matter that is essential to the gospel?

Are you looking down on or judging others?

Can you be convinced in your mind and allow others that same privilege?

Does the stance you're taking honor the Lord?

Is the disagreement causing hatred in you?

Are you ready to stand before the Lord and give an account of the stance you are choosing?

What truths about the people with whom you disagree are you struggling to let create togetherness born from the gospel among you: God has accepted them, your opinion about them doesn't matter to God, or they must live according to their own conscience?

Are you ready to stick with your church through seasons of agreement and disagreement, particularly when disagreements occur around issues outside the gospel? Ask God to give you a spirit of wisdom and patience to endure with the family in which He's placed you.

A little leaven leavens the whole batch of dough.
GALATIANS 5:9

The Glass House

WITH BEN & LYNLEY MANDRELL

Navigating Ministry and Life

Ministry leaders and their families live in a "glass house"— an environment where they are left vulnerable to the stress of ministry and the criticism of others and feel the spotlight on their personal weaknesses.

Lifeway's *The Glass House* is a space where ministry leaders will shed light on the challenges they often don't feel permission to talk about. Listeners who work in the trenches of church life will feel seen and gain tools to navigate ministry and life. Those who live outside this "glass house" will better understand what it's like to dwell there.

Join Ben and Lynley Mandrell for these shockingly confessional— yet redemptive—conversations.

Lifeway podcasts

Discover God's vision for the church.

The church described in Acts 2 is quite different from what most of us experience today. Has God changed? Or are we missing something?

This study of the early church offers some powerful insights on commitment, fellowship, prayer, giving, unity, and more. Observing the common practices of the first believers can inspire us to pursue a deeper connection to God and His mission.

- See yourself as a member of the family of God, where you are known and loved.
- Experience depth within community.
- Learn to give your life away in service to Jesus and others.
- Help your church become a blessing to your city.
- Maintain the unity of the body in shared commitment and mission.

STUDYING ON YOUR OWN?

To enrich your study experience, be sure to access the videos available through a redemption code printed in this *Bible Study Book*.

LEADING A GROUP?

Each group member will need a *Together Bible Study Book*, which includes video access. Because all participants will have access to the video content, you can choose to watch the videos outside of your group meeting if desired. Or, if you're watching together and someone misses a group meeting, they'll have the flexibility to catch up.

TOGETHER

COMMUNITY THAT MARKED
THE ACTS 2 CHURCH

Here's Your Video Access

To stream the Bible study teaching videos, follow these steps:

1. Go to my.lifeway.com/redeem and register or log in to your Lifeway account.

2. Enter this redemption code to gain access to your individual-use video license:

4Y95S7M8Q9S5

Once you've entered your personal redemption code, stream the Bible study teaching videos any time from your Digital Library page on my.lifeway.com or watch them via the Lifeway On Demand app on a compatible TV or mobile device via your Lifeway account. No need to enter your code more than once! To watch your streaming videos, just log in to your Lifeway account at my.lifeway.com or watch using the Lifeway On Demand app.

Slow or unreliable internet connection? Videos can be downloaded to your device so you can play them offline. Simply download your videos on the Lifeway On Demand app when you are in a place with strong internet connection. Then, you'll be able to watch your session videos anywhere, any time. Look for the download symbol beside your video.

QUESTIONS? WE HAVE ANSWERS!
Visit support.lifeway.com and search "Video Redemption Code" or
"Video Streaming FAQ" or call our Tech Support Team at 866.627.8553.